THE SHINING MOMENTS

Published by POCKET BOOKS, INC.

COPYRIGHT, ©, 1964 BY GERALD GARDNER.
ALL RIGHTS RESERVED. PUBLISHED ON
THE SAME DAY IN CANADA BY POCKET
BOOKS OF CANADA, LTD., MONTREAL.
PRINTED IN THE U.S.A...

PHOTOGRAPHS COURTESY WIDE WORLD PHOTOS
AND UNITED PRESS INTERNATIONAL

THE
SHINING MOMENTS
THE WORDS AND MOODS
OF John F. Kennedy

With the Memorial Tribute of Adlai E. Stevenson

Edited by GERALD GARDNER

"Today we mourn him...

tomorrow we shall miss him."

PRESIDENT KENNEDY was so contemporary a man—so involved in our world — so immersed in our times — so responsive to its challenges — so intense a participant in the great events and great decisions of our day, that he seemed the very symbol of the vitality and exuberance that is the essence of life itself.

Never once did he lose his way in the maze; never once did he falter in the storm of spears; never once was he intimidated. Like the ancient prophets he loved the people enough to warn them of their errors. And the man who loves his country best will hold it to its highest standards. He made us proud to be Americans....

We shall not soon forget that as the leader of a great nation he met and mastered his responsibility to wield great power with great restraint. "Our national strength matters," he said, "but the spirit which informs, and controls, our strength matters just as much."

We shall not soon forget that he held fast to a vision of a world in which the peace is secure; in which inevitable conflicts are reconciled by pacific means; in which nations devote their energies to the welfare of all their citizens; and in which the cast and colorful diversity of human society can flourish in a restless, competitive search for a better society.

We shall not soon forget that by word and by deed he gave proof of profound confidence in the present value and the future promise of the United Nations.

And we shall never forget these ambitions, these visions, these convictions that so inspired this remarkable young man and so quickened the quality and tempo of our times in these fleeting past three years. And our grief is compounded by the bitter irony that he who gave his all to contain violence, lost his all — to violence.

Now he is gone. Today we mourn him. Tomorrow and tomorrow we shall miss him. And so we shall never know how different the world might have been had fate permitted this blazing talent to live and labor longer at man's unfinished agenda for peace and progress for all....

A TRIBUTE BY

Adlai E. Stevenson

November 27, 1963

"OUR NATIONAL PURPOSE

IS NOT MERELY TO SURVIVE

BUT TO PREVAIL."

"I do not believe that any of us would

exchange places with any other people or any other generation.

The energy, the faith, the devotion

which we bring to this endeavor

will light our country and all who serve it —

and the glow from that fire

can truly light the world."

"*We do not want to fight —*

but we have fought before."

"Every time we deny to one of our citizens the right of equality of opportunity before the law, the right to send their children to schools on the basis of equality, so much weaker are we in Africa, Asia and Latin America, where we are a white minority in a colored world."

"Though Mr. Khrushchev may claim that his nation, like ours, is also a home of the brave, this nation — not Russia — is still the land of the free. And that, in the last analysis, is going to make the difference."

"While we shall negotiate freely, we shall not negotiate freedom."

"Since this country was founded, each generation of Americans has been summoned to give testimony to its national loyalty. The graves of young Americans who answered the call to service surround the globe."

"We cannot hope to escape a prolonged and powerful competition with Soviet power — a competition which demands that we act from enlightened impulses but never act impulsively."

"If you prefer more effective detergents or longer tail fins over sending technicians to Latin America . . . if you scoff at intellectuals, harass scientists, and reward only athletic achievements, then the future is very dark indeed."

"I call upon all of you

to join us in a journey to the new frontier.

The voyage is a long and hazardous one,

but we are all partners

in a great and historic journey."

"I am the man who accompanied Jacqueline Kennedy to Paris."

"We meet here in an hour of grief and challenge. Dag Hammarskjöld is dead. But the United Nations lives. The problem is not the death of one man — the problem is the life of this organization. It will either grow to meet the challenges of our age or it will be gone with the wind, without influence, without force, without respect."

"Until all the powerful are just, the weak will be secure only in the strength of the General Assembly."

"Let us begin anew — remembering on both sides that civility is not a sign of weakness, and sincerity is always subject to proof. Let us never negotiate out of fear. But let us never fear to negotiate."

"If a beachhead of cooperation may push back the jungle of suspicion, let both sides join in creating a new endeavor, not a new balance of power, but a new world of law, where the strong are just and the weak secure and the peace preserved."

"Hungry men and women cannot wait for economic discussions or diplomatic meetings — and their hunger rests heavily on the consciences of their fellow men."

"I don't think, really, in any sense, the United Nations has failed as a concept. I think occasionally we fail it."

*"I do not promise to consider race or religion in my appointments.
I promise only that I will not consider them."*

"The hour is late — but the agenda is long."

"I believe it is important that this country sail and not lie still in the harbor."

"*I believe in an America where every family can live in a decent home in a decent neighborhood — where children can play in parks and playgrounds, not the streets of slums — where no home is unsafe or unsanitary — where a good doctor and a good hospital are neither too far away nor too expensive — and where the water is clean and the air is pure and the streets are safe at night.*"

"Two thousand years ago, after the battle of

Thermopylae, where three hundred Spartans were wiped

out by all the Persians, they carved above the graves

a sign in the rock which said, 'Passerby: Tell Sparta

we fell faithful to her service.'"

"*I believe in an America where religious intolerance will someday end — where all men and all churches are treated as equal — where every man has the same right to attend or not attend the church of his choice. This is the kind of America I believe in — and this is the kind I fought for in the South Pacific, and the kind my brother died for in Europe.*"

"I don't say history repeats itself, but I do think there is a somber lesson in history."

"We shall be judged more by what we do at home than what we preach abroad."

"If we are successful — if our effort is bold and determined enough — then the close of this decade will mark the beginning of a new era in the American experience."

"When President Roosevelt was running for a second term ... some garment workers unfolded a great sign that said, 'We love him for the enemies he has made.' Well, I have been making some good enemies lately."

"Others may confine themselves to debate, discussion and that ultimate luxury — free advice. Our responsibility is one of decision, for to govern is to choose."

"Harry Truman once said there are fourteen or fifteen million Americans who have the resources to have representatives in Washington to protect their interests, and that the interests of the great mass of other people, the hundred and fifty or sixty million, is the responsibility of the President of the United States. And I propose to fulfill it."

"It has recently been suggested that, whether I serve one or two terms in the Presidency, I will find myself at the end of that period at what might be called the awkward age — too old to begin a new career and too young to write my memoirs."

"I hear it said that West Berlin

is militarily untenable —

and so was Bastogne,

and so, in fact, was Stalingrad."

"We are one hundred eighty million different people,

with very different ideas on what we should do, and how

this country should be run, and where we should go,

and what are our responsibilities and obligations.

I think it is important that we recognize how often we

worked together to accomplish great results."

"As Americans know from our history, on our old frontier, gun battles are caused by outlaws, and not by officers of the peace."

"Terror is not a new weapon. Throughout history it has been used by those who could not prevail either by persuasion or example. But inevitably they fail, either because men are not afraid to die for a life worth living, or because the terrorists themselves come to realize that free men cannot be frightened by threats and that aggression would meet its own response."

"We are Americans. That is a proud boast. That is a great privilege, to be a citizen of the United States, and we must meet our responsibilities."

"I believe that there can only be one possible defense policy for the United States. It can be expressed in one word. That word is FIRST. I do not mean first, but. I do not mean first, when. I do not mean first, if. I mean first—period."

"I believe in an America that is on the march —

an America respected by all nations, friends and foes alike

— an America that is moving, choosing, doing, dreaming —

a strong America in a world of peace."

"Let it be recognized that this Administration recognizes

the value of dissent and daring, that we greet

healthy controversy as the hallmark of healthy change."

"It is the fate of this generation

to live with a struggle we did not start,

in a world we did not make.

But the pressures of life are not always distributed by choice.

And while no nation has ever faced such a challenge,

no nation has ever been so ready to seize

the burden and the glory of freedom."

"Let the word go forth from this time and place,

to friend and foe alike, that the torch has been passed

to a new generation of Americans — born in this century,

tempered by war, disciplined by a hard and bitter peace,

proud of our ancient heritage — and unwilling to

witness or permit the slow undoing of human rights

to which this nation has always been committed."

"The white race is in the minority, the free-enterprise system is in the minority, and the majority are looking at us harder and longer than they ever looked before."

"Our responsibility is not discharged by an announcement of virtuous ends."

"Now the trumpet summons us again — not as a call to bear arms, though arms we need — not as a call to battle, though embattled we are — but a call to bear the burden of a long twilight struggle, year in and year out, 'rejoicing in hope, patient in tribulations' — a struggle against the common enemies of man: tyranny, poverty, disease and war itself."

"Let us not seek the Republican answer or the Democratic answer but the right answer."

"Before my term has ended, we shall have tested anew whether a nation organized and governed such as ours can endure. The outcome is by no means certain. The answers are by no means clear."

"There is an old Chinese saying that each generation builds a road for the next. The road has been well built for us, and I believe it incumbent upon us, in our generation, to build our road for the next generation."

"I am glad to be here because I feel a sense of kinship

with the Pittsburgh Pirates. Like my candidacy,

they were not given much chance in the spring."

"Mr. Khrushchev may have known his Marx — but his Marx did not know the United States of America."

"A moment of pause is not a promise of peace."

"We seek not the world-wide victory of one nation or system but a world-wide victory of man. The modern globe is too small, its weapons too destructive, and its disorders too contagious to permit any other kind of victory."

"This is a great country. It can be greater. It is a powerful country. It can be more powerful."

"With a good conscience our only sure reward, with history the final judge of our deeds, let us go forth to lead the land we love, asking His blessing and His help, but knowing that here on earth God's work must truly be our own."

"I believe in an America where every child is educated, not according to his means or his race, but according to his capacity — where there are no literacy tests for voting that mean anything because there are no illiterate citizens."

"I believe in human dignity as the source of national

purpose, human liberty as the source of national action,

the human heart as the source of national compassion, and

in the human mind as the source of our invention

and our ideas."

"We are not afraid

to entrust the American people with unpleasant facts,

foreign ideas, alien philosophies and competitive values.

For a nation that is afraid

to let its people judge the truth and falsehood

in an open market

is a nation that is afraid of its people."

"When written in Chinese, the word 'crisis' is composed of two characters — one represents danger and one represents opportunity."

"Man holds in his mortal hands the power to abolish all forms of human poverty and all forms of human life."

"Let every nation know, whether it wishes us well or ill, that we shall pay any price, bear any burden, meet any hardship, support any friend, oppose any foe to assure the survival and the success of liberty."

"We will at all times be ready to talk, if talk will help. But we must also be ready to resist with force, if force is used upon us."

"Never have the nations of the world had so much to lose or so much to gain. Together we shall save our planet or together we shall perish in its flames."

"However close we sometimes seem to that dark and final abyss, let no man of peace and freedom despair. For he does not stand alone."

"To those old allies whose cultural and spiritual origins we share, we pledge the loyalty of faithful friends. United, there is little we cannot do. Divided, there is little we can do—for we dare not meet a powerful challenge at odds and split asunder."

"Let me then make it clear as the President of the United States

that I am determined upon our system's survival and success,

regardless of the cost

and regardless of the peril."

"In the long history of the world, only a few generations have been granted the role of defending freedom in its hour of maximum danger. I do not shrink from this responsibility—I welcome it."

"The hour of decision has arrived. We cannot afford to 'wait and see what happens,' while the tide of events sweeps over and beyond us. We must use time as a tool, not as a couch."

"Today, every inhabitant of this planet must contemplate the day when this planet may no longer be habitable. Every man, woman and child lives under a nuclear Sword of Damocles, hanging by the slenderest of threads, capable of being cut at any moment by accident, or miscalculation or by madness."

"When the youngest child alive today has grown to the cares

of manhood, our position in the world will be determined

first of all by what provisions we make today—

for his education, his health, and his opportunities for

a good home and a good job and a good life."

"We cannot be satisfied to rest here. This is the side of the hill, not the top. The mere absence of war is not peace. The mere absence of recession is not growth. We have made a beginning —but we have only begun."

"Of those to whom much is given, much is required."

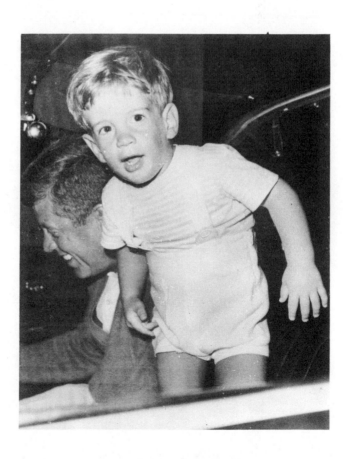

"I would rather be accused of breaking precedents

than breaking promises."

"Ask not what your country can do for you —

ask what you can do for your country."

"Our task now is not to fix the blame for the past, but to fix a course for the future."

I HAD READ every word he spoke and seen every photograph. Both revealed the man so well: the sparkling words so full of wit and bite and vision, with no time for nonsense because a nation was in peril.

And the pictures. The thousands and thousands of pictures from the wire services. Pictures in crowds. Pictures addressing august bodies. Pictures on trips. Pictures with the radiant Jacqueline. The ruminative pictures alone. The rollicking ones with others.

The words were for a book of quotations I edited. When he heard it had a modest sale, he said to me on the day I met him, "Well, it will take a little time before the words take on a greater importance." How soon he could not have guessed.

The pictures were for those captioned photo books about which he said to me, "So very funny, Gerry. I especially liked the one—"

And now he is gone. One reads and nods silently when Schlesinger and Warren and the rest tell us that, though gone, he has changed us, and we will bear his mark to our dying day. What a meager consolation for such a loss. A loss for America and for the world, yes. But what a personal loss. Never to see the ironic smile as he parried a press conference questioner. Never the clarion words as he savored a phrase that pleased him . . . .

This book is a combination of the words and the pictures. It is a curious marriage and yet a fitting one. It is curious because there is a divided target —the pictures touch one's heart while the words touch one's mind. It is fitting because, when one listened to a Kennedy speech, did not the words compel us to act, while the youthful image—how much older it grew in just three years—engaged our affection?

Now an era has come crashing to an end. The sense of feeling fully alive and alert in an age of challenge is somehow gone. And the man who tried to draw the poison from our society is struck down by its violence.

One's first reaction—after the certainty that this cannot possibly be true—is a disgust with the men who, though they pulled no trigger, harbored the same hatred for this golden man, and mocked and slandered and frustrated him. One's first reaction is a sense of futility and waste that the most gifted and promising of men should be cut down at the height of his powers.

This is one's first reaction. It is said that death teaches us a sad truth—not that one mourns so long but that one forgets so soon. I suspect this will not be the case. I suspect that, though this first reaction of fury and pain will diminish as other emergencies engage us, there is a permanent part of many of us that is numbed and dead along with John F. Kennedy.

Gerald Gardner